Christmas Crafts:

Easy Christmas Crafts Anyone Can Make!

Barb Asselin

Asselin Group Online Publisher
R.R. #2, 449 Flat Rapids Road
Arnprior, ON Canada K7S 3G8

www.AsselinGroup.com

Copyright © 2014 Barb Asselin
First Printed November 16, 2014

All Rights reserved. No part of this book may be reproduced or used in any way or form or by any means whether electronic or mechanical, this means that you cannot record or photocopy any material ideas or text or graphics that are provided in this book.

ALSO BY BARB ASSELIN

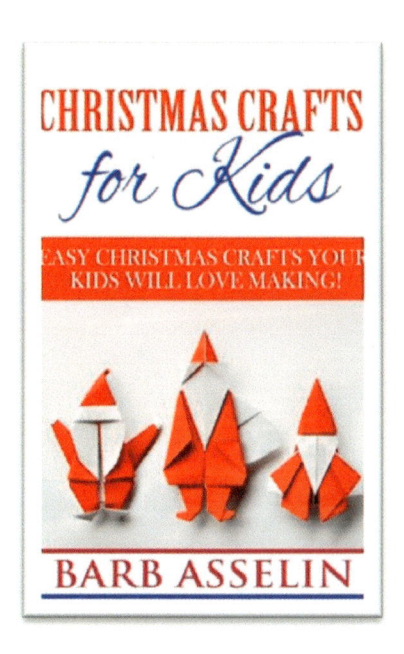

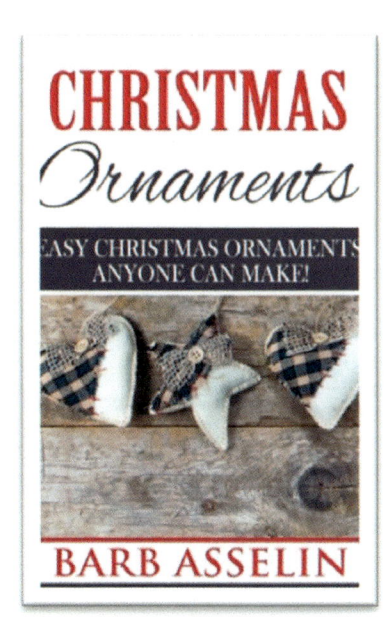

ABOUT THE AUTHOR

Barb Asselin is a college professor and best-selling author who has published books in many different genres including education, cooking, crafts, law, real estate, internet marketing, entrepreneurship, baby sign language, fitness, office administration, children's fiction and children's non-fiction.

Barb loves crafts and can often be found with her two daughters in her "craft room" finding a new project to either start or complete. She has been crocheting since her Nanny Short taught her how to chain while she was in grade school.

Since she began teaching in 2004, Barb has taught in six different programs within the School of Business and has created numerous online courses for Algonquin College including the Virtual Assistant program.

She loves to teach through her courses, books, and textbooks, and strives to make a connection with each student and reader. Barb lives in Canada with her husband, Mike, and two adorable daughters, Casey and Jamie. They enjoy music, skiing, golfing, running, and mixed martial arts.

WHY YOU SHOULD READ THIS BOOK

Do you love to make Christmas crafts but think you have already done it all?

Do you like the idea of making Christmas crafts, but think they may be too hard?

Do you love the Christmas holidays but struggle to find fun things to do with your kids to celebrate?

Do you have children who love to do crafts but they keep making the same crafts each year?

Would you like to find some fun and easy crafts to make this holiday season?

Want to get your kids away from the computer for a little bit?

Would you like to make some wonderful handmade gifts to give to friends, family members, and teachers?

Do you love Christmas and can't wait to make new crafts each year?

Do you teach children or have a home day care or grandchildren that you would love to plan some fun crafts with?

This book is filled with fun and easy crafts that can be made by you, your friends, and your children (note some will require adult supervision). Inside you will find many Christmas crafts, tree ornaments, and even some easy handmade gift ideas for some special people on your Christmas list.

There are crafts inside that are great for moms, dads, kids, people with sewing experience, people with woodworking experience, people with no crafting experience, and even families working together!

With this book, you can make:

- Cookie Garland
- Gingerbread House
- Wooden Snowman #1
- Wooden Snowman #2
- Wooden Snowman #3
- Angel Ornament
- Apple Cider Mix
- Wooden XMAS Letters
- Wooden Sucker Christmas Tree
- Candle Centerpiece
- Christmas Stockings
- Pinecone Wreath
- Evergreen Wreath
- Mug O' Gingerbread Men
- Sugar Cookie Christmas Trees
- Painted Pinecones
- Cookie Mix Jar

Are you ready to make some fun and easy crafts this holiday season? Let's get started…

CHRISTMAS CRAFTS:
EASY CHRISTMAS CRAFTS ANYONE CAN MAKE!

TABLE OF CONTENTS

Also by Barb Asselin 3

About the Author 5

Why You Should Read This Book 7

Introduction 11

Cookie Garland 13

Gingerbread House 15

Wooden Snowman #1 19

Wooden Snowman #2 21

Wooden Snowman #3 23

Angel Ornament 25

Apple Cider Mix (Great for Gifts!) 27

Wooden XMAS Letters 29

Wooden Sucker Christmas Tree 31

Candle Centerpiece 35

Christmas Stockings 37

Pinecone Wreath.. 39

Evergreen Wreath 41

Mug O' Gingerbread Men (Great for Gifts!) 43

Sugar Cookie Christmas Trees.. 47

Painted Pinecones 51

Oatmeal Chocolate Chip Cookie Mix Jar............................ 53

Conclusion 57

Other Craft Books by Barb Asselin...................................... 59

Cookbooks by Barb Asselin 60

Enjoy this book?.. 61

INTRODUCTION

Thank you for downloading this book and supporting an independent author. I really appreciate it.

I have always loved making crafts. As a kid, I learned how to crochet from my Nanny Short when I was just young. Now that I have two daughters of my own, we spend lots of time making crafts, researching how to do a certain craft, or even making our own greeting cards, and gifts.

Not only do I love making crafts, but Christmas is one of my favorite times of the year. I love the whole season leading up to Christmas. I usually start in mid-October with baking all of my family's favorite Christmas treats. I load up the freezer full of yummy desserts and then take a tray of mixed cookies, chocolates, and squares to everyone's house that we visit during the holidays.

Every Christmas, my daughters and I plan what we will give each person as a Christmas present and think of gifts that we can make ourselves. We spend our fall weekends making gifts for others or making Christmas ornaments for our tree. We have so much fun!

I hope you will enjoy some fun crafting days either on your own, with some friends, or with the children in your life this year. **Note that, if you are planning to make some of these crafts with children, some of these projects will require some assistance or supervision by an adult or an older child. Note also that four of these projects require some basic wood working skills, such as cutting**

wood with an axe, or a table saw, or using a drill to drill some holes into some wood pieces.

My goal was to create a book that would appeal to all types of crafters and future crafters:

- people with cooking or baking experience
- people with woodworking experience
- people with sewing experience
- even people with no crafting experience!

I hope you enjoy and try something new and maybe even try a craft that is outside of your comfort level. Happy crafting!

Christmas Crafts

COOKIE GARLAND

Materials:

- Star cookie cutter
- Drinking straw
- White fabric paint
- 1 recipe salt dough
    - 2 cups flour
    - 1 cup salt
    - 1/2 cup allspice or cinnamon
    - 2 teaspoons wallpaper paste
    - 1/2 cup water
- Polyurethane varnish
- Approximately 10-15' of seasonal rope ribbon

Instructions:

- Preheat oven to 250F
- Combine all salt dough ingredients and knead until smooth
- Roll out dough to 1/4" to 1/2" thick
- Cut out 14 star shapes using the cookie cutter
- Use a straw to cut a hole out of the top of each star shape for hanging
- Place on ungreased baking tray and bake for one hour
- Turn and bake for another hour
- Turn oven off and let shapes cool in oven
- Varnish with polyurethane
- Write MERRY CHRISTMAS by putting 1 letter on each cookie with white fabric paint
- Thread a length of ribbon through the hole at the top of each cookie and create a garland to hang in a doorway or on a Christmas tree

Makes 1 "Merry Christmas" garland

Gingerbread House

Materials:

- Gingerbread Dough recipe (see below)
- Icing recipe (see below)
- Tree cookie cutter
- Rolling pin
- Sharp knife
- Large platter or foil covered piece of cardboard
- Candies for decorating

Instructions:

- Make 1 batch of gingerbread dough
- Make 1 batch of royal icing
- Follow instructions below for cutting out gingerbread house and trees
- Decorate with icing and candies

- Display on tray or foil wrapped piece of cardboard

Gingerbread Dough Ingredients:

- 1c brown sugar
- 1/3 c butter or margarine
- 1 ½ c dark molasses
- 2/3 c cold water
- 7c flour
- 2t baking soda
- 2t ground ginger
- 1t salt
- 1t ground allspice
- 1t ground cloves
- 1t ground cinnamon

Instructions:

Preheat oven to 350 degrees. Cream the brown sugar and butter together in a large bowl. Add molasses and water and combine. Mix dry ingredients together and add slowly, combining as you go, until it is all mixed together. Form into a ball and refrigerate for at least 2 hours. Roll dough on floured surface to 1/2" thick and cut according to the following diagram using a sharp knife:

Christmas Crafts

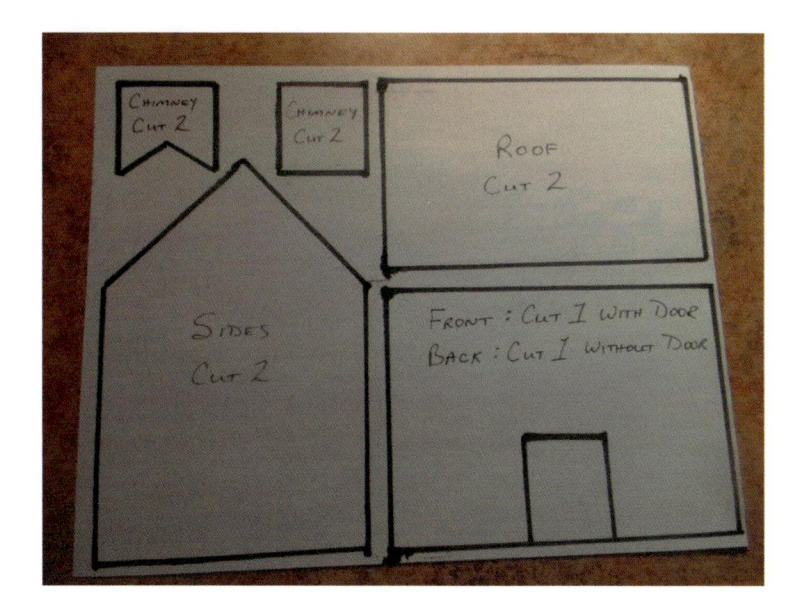

Cut remaining dough into gingerbread trees with cookie cutter. Place on ungreased baking sheet about 2 inches apart. Bake for 10-12 minutes until no indentation remains when touched. Cool on cookie racks. Decorate with frosting and candies as desired using icing as glue to hold your gingerbread house together.

Royal Icing:

- 2 egg whites
- 3 cups of icing or powdered sugar
- 1/2 teaspoon of cream of tartar
- 2 tablespoons of lemon juice

Mix the icing sugar with the cream of tartar. Mix the powdered mixture into the egg whites a little at a time until you have almost added all of it. Then mix in the lemon juice. Finally, add the rest of the powdered mixture. You want the icing to be the consistency of soft ice cream or mashed potatoes, so add more icing sugar if you need. If it is too thick, add a bit more lemon juice. Decorate.

Makes 1 gingerbread house with accessories

Christmas Crafts 19

WOODEN SNOWMAN #1

Materials:

Note that this project will require some woodwork and potentially the use of an axe or a band saw or a table saw to cut the wood pieces.

- 4 wooden logs, approximately 6" in diameter and 6-8" long
- 2 small wooden branches, approximately 1" in diameter and 6" long, with one end cut on an angle
- 1 peeled carrot

- 5 black buttons, 1" in diameter
- 2" slice of wooden log, approximately 8-10" in diameter
- White spray paint
- Black spray paint
- Red spray paint
- Wood glue

Instructions:

- Spray paint one of the wooden logs black
- Spray paint the 2" slice of wooden log black
- Slice an end off of each of the remaining three wooden logs, so that they will stack one on top of the other and the bottom one will sit flat on the ground (with adult supervision)
- Spray paint the three remaining wooden logs white
- Spray paint the two wooden sticks red
- Let paint dry
- Stack the three white logs one on top of the other and glue in place
- Glue the two red sticks on as arms
- Glue the 2" slice of log on top as the brim of the snowman's hat
- Glue the black log on top as the rest of the hat
- Glue the buttons on as eyes and buttons
- Glue the carrot on as the nose (note that you may need to drill a hole for the carrot to sit in, or use a nail)

Makes 1 snowman

Christmas Crafts 21

Wooden Snowman #2

Note that this project will require some woodwork and potentially the use of an axe or a band saw or a table saw or a wood plane to cut the wood pieces.

Materials:

- 1 piece of wood, 4" x 4", approximately 24" long
- 1 wooden circle, 1/2" thick and approximately 6-8" in diameter
- 1 wooden dowel, 2" in diameter and 4" long
- Piece of carrot
- Black permanent marker
- Wood glue
- 3 buttons, approximately 1 or 1 1/2" in diameter
- Length of fabric, approximately 18" long and 2-3" wide
- 2 branches with a "Y" shape at one end
- Flat thumb tack

- Finishing nail and hammer (optional)
- White acrylic paint
- Paint brush
- Black spray paint

Instructions:

- Using a wood plane or a table saw or an axe (with adult supervision), chamfer or bevel the edges of the wooden 4 x 4
- Spray paint the wooden dowel and the wooden circle black
- Use the white paint to paint the flat edges of the wooden 4 x 4
- Use the white paint to paint diagonal lines on the bevelled edges of the wooden 4 x 4
- Let paint dry
- Glue the wooden circle on top of the 4 x 4
- Glue the wooden dowel on top of the wooden circle to make the hat
- Glue the two branches on the back of the snowman as arms
- Wrap the fabric around the arms to secure and fasten in the front with the thumb tack
- Use the permanent marker to draw the snowman's face
- Glue the buttons on the front of the snowman
- Attach the carrot as the snowman's nose with a nail or glue

Makes 1 snowman

Christmas Crafts 23

Wooden Snowman #3

Note that this project will require some woodwork and potentially the use of a band saw or a table saw to cut the wood pieces.

Materials:

- Wooden rectangles, as follows:
    - 12" x 6" x 2" (base)
    - 10" x 5" x 2" (bottom)
    - 8" x 4" x 2" (middle)
    - 6" x 3" x 2" (face)
    - 7" x 4" x 1" (brim)
    - 4" x 3" x 2" (hat)
- White spray paint
- Black spray paint
- Black acrylic paint

- Orange acrylic paint
- Paint brush
- Wood glue
- Piece of felt or fabric for scarf, approximately 36" long and 3" wide

Instructions:

- Spray paint the following pieces white:
  - Base
  - Bottom
  - Middle
  - Face
- Spray paint the following pieces black:
  - Brim
  - Hat
- Let paint dry
- Use wood glue to glue the pieces together in the following order from bottom to top:
  - Base
  - Bottom
  - Middle
  - Face
  - Brim
  - Hat
- Paint the face of the snowman
- Tie the scarf around the middle section of the snowman

Makes 1 snowman

Christmas Crafts 25

ANGEL ORNAMENT

Materials:

- Two sheets of foil paper (8 1/2" x 11"), 1 each of golf and blue (or any other colors you may choose)
- 1 small wooden ball with a hole in the center
- 1 small piece of wooden dowel to fit in the hole in the wooden ball, approximately 1-2" long
- 2-4 feathers
- Small amount of doll hair
- Piece of embroidery thread, approximately 6-8" long

- White glue
- Hole punch

Instructions:

- The gold piece of foil paper will be used at its regular size
- Cut 2" off the length of the other piece of foil paper so that it is 6 1/2" x 11"
- Fold each piece of foil paper into a fan on the long side, by placing the long side in front of you on a table and folding into 1" folds (1 up, 1 down) until you reach the end of each piece of paper
- With the gold foil showing on the outside, fold the gold fan in half lengthwise
- Use the hole punch to punch a hole in the middle
- Fold the smaller piece of foil paper in half lengthwise
- Use the hole punch to punch a hole in the middle of that piece as well
- Glue the dowel into the hole in the wooden ball
- Thread the dowel into the hole in the colored foil fan and then into the hole in the gold foil fan
- Glue the paper into place on the dowel
- Glue the feathers on the back of the angel as wings
- Tie the embroidery thread around the neck of the angel and tie in a bow or a knot for hanging
- Finally, glue the hair onto the angel's head
- Let the glue dry and then hang on your tree

Makes 1 angel

Apple Cider Mix (Great for Gifts!)

Materials:

- 2 c empty mason jar with lid
- 1 1/4 cups of dark brown sugar
- 2 tablespoons each of:
    - Ground ginger
    - Ground cloves
    - Ground cinnamon
    - Ground nutmeg
    - Ground allspice

- Piece of cardstock
- Festive permanent marker
- Hole punch
- Ribbon, approximately 10-12" long
- Brown sugar "keeper" (optional

Instructions:

- Mix all ingredients together and put in jar
- Add brown sugar keeper to keep mixture moist
- Use marker to write instructions on cardstock (or type on computer and print out)

> Delicious Apple Cider
> Mix 1-2 tablespoons of this mixture into a cup of apple juice
> Heat and enjoy!

- Punch a hole in the top left corner of your paper
- Attach instructions to jar with ribbon

Makes 1 gift

Christmas Crafts

WOODEN XMAS LETTERS

Materials:

- Wooden letters from craft store:
    - X, M, A, and S
- White spray paint
- Gold acrylic paint
- Nail file or piece of sand paper
- Sponge
- 2 buttons
- 2 sleigh bells
- Small amounts of red fabric
- Small amounts of pattered fabric
- White glue
- Needle and matching thread or sewing machine

Instructions:

- Spray paint the letters white
- Rough the edges of the letters with the sand paper or nail file
- Use the sponge to apply gold paint on the roughed edges

- Cut two strips of patterned material, approximately 1" x 6"
- Fold strips into a bow and glue onto the X and the A
- Glue a button to the center of each bow
- Cut two triangles from the red material, 6" wide and 6" long
- Cut two strips of patterned material, approximately 6" long and 3" wide
- Using either a needle and thread or a sewing machine, sew two sides of the triangle together
- Turn right side out and trim bottom so that it is not on an angle (fold it flat with the seam in the back and trim the bottom half to match the top half)
- Next, sew the rectangular piece of material to the bottom of the hat, for the brim
- Flip the rectangular piece of material up so that it covers the seam you just created
- Sew a sleigh bell to the end of the hat
- Repeat to make a second hat
- Glue the hats to the top right corners of the M and the S

Makes 1 gift or centrepiece

Wooden Sucker Christmas Tree

Note that this project will require some woodwork and potentially the use of a band saw or a table saw to cut the wood pieces and the use of a drill to drill holes in the wood.

Materials:

- 23-1" x 1" pieces of wood, in the following lengths:
    - 2 pieces 12" long
    - 2 pieces 11" long
    - 2 pieces 10" long
    - 2 pieces 9" long
    - 2 pieces 8" long
    - 2 pieces 7" long

- 2 pieces 6" long
- 2 pieces 5" long
- 2 pieces 4" long
- 2 pieces 3" long
- 2 pieces 2" long
- 1 piece 1" long
- 1 wooden base, 4" x 4" square, 1" thick, or 4" in diameter
- Green spray paint
- 3/8" dowel, 24" long
- 3/8" drill bit
- 1/8" drill bit
- 45 suckers
- Polyurethane varnish
- Paint brush
- Wood glue

Instructions:

- Varnish the base with at least 2 coats of varnish
- Spray paint the 23 wooden pieces green
- Using the drill and the 3/8" drill bit, drill a hole through the center of each of the 22 longest pieces of wood, as well as the base
- Drill a 3/8" hole through half of the 1" piece of wood
- Drill a 1/8" hole through the other half of the 1" piece of wood, so that there is a 1/8" hole on one side and a 3/8" hole on the other side and they meet in the middle
- Using the drill and the 1/8" drill bit, drill a hole at each end of each of the 22 longest pieces, 1/2" from each end, for the suckers

Christmas Crafts

- Starting with the base and the dowel, build your tree as follows:
    - Glue the dowel into the base
    - Thread the two 12" pieces of wood onto the dowel, turning them so that they are perpendicular to each other
    - Add the two 11" pieces of wood, turning them so that each one is offset from the one below it
    - Add the two 10" pieces of wood, turning them so that each one is offset from the one below it
    - Add the two 9" pieces of wood, turning them so that each one is offset from the one below it
    - Add the two 8" pieces of wood, turning them so that each one is offset from the one below it
    - Add the two 7" pieces of wood, turning them so that each one is offset from the one below it
    - Add the two 6" pieces of wood, turning them so that each one is offset from the one below it
    - Add the two 5" pieces of wood, turning them so that each one is offset from the one below it
    - Add the two 4" pieces of wood, turning them so that each one is offset from the one below it
    - Add the two 3" pieces of wood, turning them so that each one is offset from the one below it
    - Add the two 2" pieces of wood, turning them so that each one is offset from the one below it
    - Add the 1" piece of wood to the top of the tree
- Add suckers to the ends of each tree branch and to the top of the tree

Makes 1 tree

Candle Centerpiece

Materials:

- Styrofoam ring, 12" in diameter and 1-2" wide and 1/2-1" thick
- 4 round, red candles, 3" in diameter
- Approximately 150-200 small pinecones
- A few sprigs of artificial spruce tree
- A few sprigs of artificial berries
- 20-30 red balls in various sizes
- 6-8 cinnamon sticks, broken in half
- Hot glue gun and glue sticks

Instructions:

- Using glue sticks, cover Styrofoam ring with pinecones

- Glue on the four red candles so that they are evenly spaced throughout the circle
- Add the red glass balls, spruce sprigs, berries, and cinnamon sticks until project is finished

Makes 1 centerpiece

Christmas Stockings

Materials:

- White piece of felt, approximately 12" x 36"
- Red piece of felt, approximately 12" x 36"
- Red and white embroidery thread and needle
- Small amounts of white and red felt
- 2 pieces of red ribbon, approximately 6-8" long each
- White and red fabric paint (optional)

Instructions:

- Fold the red felt in half so that it is 12" x 18"
- Draw and cut two stockings from the folded felt, basing the shape on the photo above
- Repeat for the white felt
- Cut 1 white heart and 1 red heart from the leftover felt

- Use white embroidery thread on the red heart and red embroidery thread on the white heart to embroider a snowflake shape onto each heart (optional) – note that another option would be to use fabric paint to paint a snowflake on each heart
- Sew each heart on the opposite color of stocking (fronts only) using a large embroidery stitch – note that you should sew the red heart with white embroidery thread and the white heart with red embroidery thread
- With wrong sides together, sew each stocking around the outside using a blanket stitch and red embroidery thread
- Fold each piece of ribbon in half and sew to the inside of each stocking

Makes 2 stockings

Pinecone Wreath

Materials:

- Wire frame for wreath, 12" in diameter
- 6 large pinecones
- 18 small-medium sized pinecones
- Gold spray paint
- 6 sprigs of spruce tree branches
- 12-18 sprigs of berries
- Hot glue gun and glue sticks
- Approximately 36" of 3" wide fabric ribbon (optional)

Instructions:

- Spray paint all pinecones with golf spray paint
- Glue large pinecones to wire frame, making sure they are equally spaced around the frame

- Glue 1 sprig of spruce branches in between each large pinecone
- Glue 3 small or medium sized pinecones in between each large pinecone
- Embellish with berry sprigs
- Tie a large bow with the fabric ribbon and attach to the top of your wreath (optional)
- Hang

Makes 1 wreath

Evergreen Wreath

Materials:

- 1 evergreen wreath
- Various colored small glass or plastic ornaments
- Approximately 24"-30" of red ribbon, 1" wide
- Three sprigs of berries
- Red and white string beads, approximately 24"-30" each
- Hot glue gun and glue sticks
- Approximately 36" of 3" wide fabric ribbon (optional)

Instructions:

- Wrap red string beads around wreath and secure with hot glue gun

- Wrap white string beads around wreath (using a different path than the white beads) and secure with hot glue gun
- Wrap the red ribbon around wreath (using a different path again) and secure with hot glue gun
- Embellish with berries sprigs and colored ornaments
- Tie a large bow with the fabric ribbon and attach to the top of your wreath (optional)
- Hang

Makes 1 wreath

Mug O' Gingerbread Men (Great for Gifts!)

Materials:

- 1 decorative/festive porcelain mug for each gift that you wish to make
- 1 sprig of artificial spruce tree for each gift that you wish to make
- 1 recipe gingerbread cookies (recipe below)
- Gingerbread man cookie cutter
- 1 recipe decorative icing (recipe below)
- Clear cellophane wrap (optional)
- 1/8" ribbon (optional)

Instructions:

- Bake two gingerbread men for each gift that you wish to make

- Arrange two gingerbread men with spruce tree sprig in festive mug
- Wrap gifts in cellophane wrap and decorate with ribbon (optional) before giving

Ingredients:

- 1c brown sugar
- 1/3 c butter or margarine
- 1 ½ c dark molasses
- 2/3 c cold water
- 7c flour
- 2t baking soda
- 2t ground ginger
- 1t salt
- 1t ground allspice
- 1t ground cloves
- 1t ground cinnamon
- White or colored frosting (optional)
- Candies (optional)

Instructions:

Preheat oven to 350 degrees. Cream the brown sugar and butter together. Add molasses and water and combine. Mix dry ingredients together and add slowly, combining as you go, until it is all mixed together. Form into a ball and refrigerate for at least 2 hours. Roll dough on floured surface to ¼ inch thick and cut with cookie cutters. Place on ungreased baking sheet about 2 inches apart. Bake for 10-12 minutes until no indentation remains when touched. Cool on cookie racks. Decorate with frosting and candies as desired.

Frosting:

Mix 1c icing sugar with 4t milk and combine until smooth. Add a dash of vanilla. Add milk or icing sugar as necessary to get desired consistency. Add food coloring as necessary. Decorate.

Sugar Cookie Christmas Trees

Materials:

- Large-sized star cookie cutter
- Medium-sized star cookie cutter
- Small-sized star cookie cutter
- Sugar cookie dough (recipe below)
- White icing (recipe below)
- Silver ball cake decorations
- White sugar or icing sugar for dusting

Ingredients:

- 1 ½ c butter, softened
- 2c white sugar
- 4 eggs
- 1t vanilla
- 5c flour
- 2t baking powder
- 1t salt

Instructions:

Preheat oven to 400 degrees. Cream the butter and sugar together in a medium-sized bowl. Add eggs and vanilla and beat with mixer until smooth. Mix dry ingredients together and add slowly until all ingredients are mixed together. Form into ball, cover, and refrigerate for at least 1 hour. Roll dough on floured surface to 1/2" thick. Cut into the following shapes:

- Each tree will require:
    - 3 large star cookies
    - 2 medium star cookies
    - 2 small star cookies

Place on ungreased baking sheet 1 inch apart. Bake for 8-10 minutes or until the edges are starting to brown. Cool on cookie rack.

Frosting:

Mix 1c icing sugar with 4t milk and combine until smooth. Add a dash of vanilla. Add milk or icing sugar as necessary to get desired consistency.

Christmas Crafts 49

Use frosting as "glue" to build trees as follows:

- Place 1 large star on the counter or a small paper plate
- Glue the second large star on top, making sure that the points of the star are off center from the previous layer
- Glue the first medium star on top, making sure that the points of the star are off center from the previous layer
- Glue the second medium star on top, making sure that the points of the star are off center from the previous layer
- Glue the first small star on top, making sure that the points of the star are off center from the previous layer
- Glue the second large star on top, making sure that the points of the star are off center from the previous layer
- Glue the last small star on top, so that it stands up like the star on top of a Christmas tree
- Embellish tree with silver ball cake decorations and sugar as a "snow" dusting

Makes approximately 12-15 trees

Christmas Crafts 51

PAINTED PINECONES

Materials:

- Various pinecones
- Acrylic paint or spray paint in desired color
- Paint brush
- Container or basket

Instructions:

- Use paint brush to paint pinecones in desired color of paint
- Alternatively, spray paint your pinecones in desired color of paint
- Let dry

- Fill a bowl or basket or glass container with your painted pinecones

Variations:

- Consider embellishing painted pinecones with glitter glue, beads, or even spray snow
- Consider painting each pinecone a different color, or use two or three "Christmasy" colors such as red, green, and gold
- Add a bow or some small glass ball ornaments to your project

Makes 1 centerpiece or decoration

Oatmeal Chocolate Chip Cookie Mix Jar

Materials:

- 1 one-quart jar with lid
- 1/3 cup white sugar
- 1/3 cup brown sugar
- 3/4 cup flour
- 1/2 teaspoon baking powder
- 1/8 teaspoon baking soda
- 1/8 teaspoon salt
- 1 cup quick cooking oatmeal
- 1 cup chocolate chips
- 12" length of ribbon
- Cardstock for baking instructions and label

- Christmas embellishments (optional)
- White glue or tape

Instructions:

- Layer all of the dry ingredients in the jar, tamping down each layer so that each layer is cleanly separated, in this order:
    - Mix together flour, oatmeal, baking soda, baking powder, and sale as the first layer
    - Brown sugar
    - White sugar
    - Chocolate chips
- Place lid on the container
- Write directions on cardstock and decorate with border or Christmas embellishments
    - Preheat oven to 375 degrees
    - Mix together 1/2 cup margarine or butter, 1 egg, and 1 teaspoon vanilla in a medium-sized bowl until mixed together well
    - Add the cookie mix from this jar to the bowl and mix together
    - Cover and cool in fridge for 30 minutes or overnight
    - Drop tablespoon-sized balls onto a cookie sheet, spaced 2" apart
    - Bake for 8-10 minutes or until edges are golden brown
    - Cool slightly on baking sheet, then remove to wire racks
    - Makes approximately 18 cookies
- Write title of cookies on cardstock and decorate with border or Christmas embellishments

- Glue or tape title to front of jar
- Punch hole in instructions
- Thread ribbon through hole in instructions and tie around the neck of the jar

Makes 1 jar gift

CONCLUSION

Congratulations on making your way through this book! I hope you enjoyed the craft ideas and have even made a few.

I also hope that you have shared these crafts with your family, friends, or the child or children in your life to make the anticipation of the holiday season that much more special. I love the whole lead-up time to the Christmas holidays because I can go through my craft room or even the recycling and find some materials to turn into some fun crafts. When the kids have their friends over, we usually bake something or I set the kids up to be creative and make a craft to take home. They love that!

Please feel free to use the ideas in this book in various different color combinations and as a starting point for creating your own unique holiday masterpieces.

Happy crafting!

OTHER CRAFT BOOKS BY BARB ASSELIN

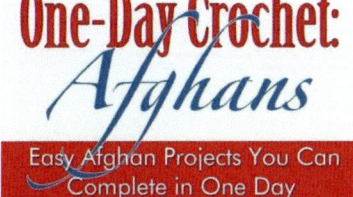

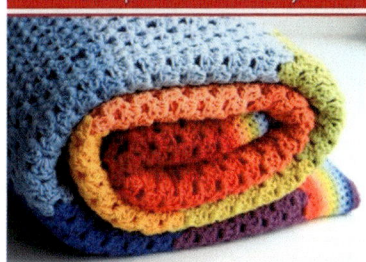

Cookbooks by Barb Asselin

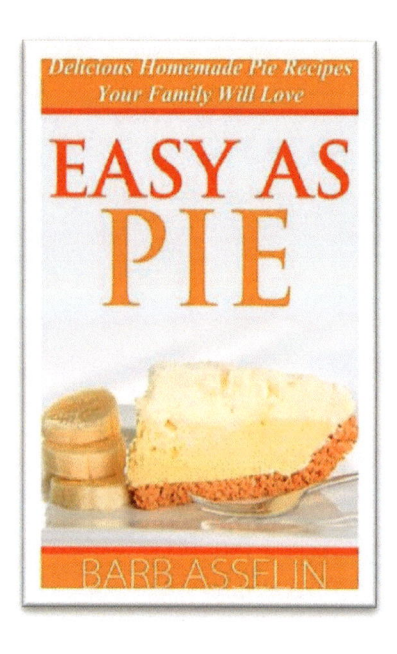

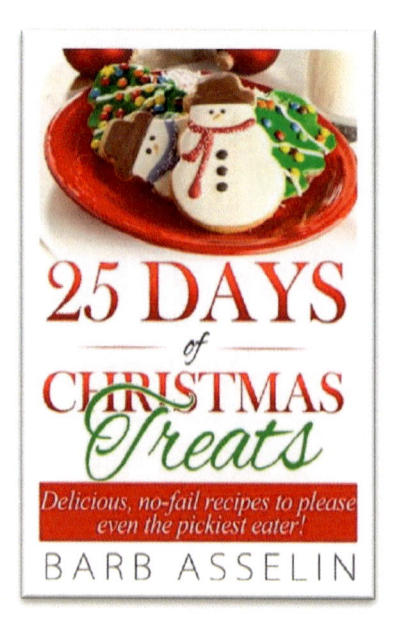

ENJOY THIS BOOK?

I see you've made it all the way to the end of my book. I'm so glad you enjoyed it enough to get all the way through! If you liked the book, would you be open to leaving me a review? You see, I'm a self-published author, and when people like you are able to give me reviews, it helps me out in a big way. You can leave a review for me at Amazon page for this book.

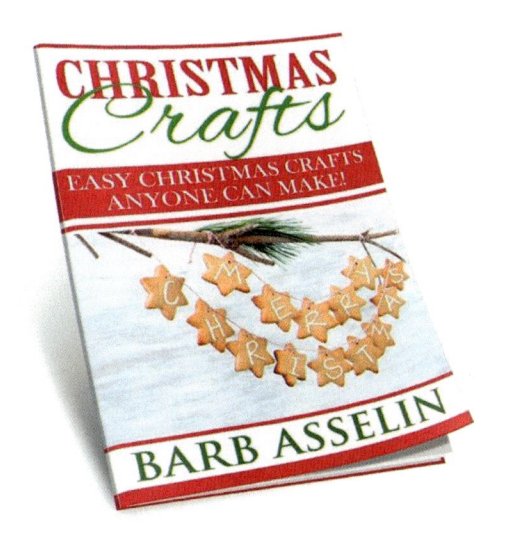

It'd really mean a lot to me.

Thank you.

Barb Asselin

Printed in Great Britain
by Amazon